ASSURED PERIODIC TENANCY AGREEMENT

AF891929

Notes for Guidance

Insert date of Agreement.

DATED ______________________________

for a furnished or unfurnished house or flat on an Assured Periodic Tenancy

WRITTEN STATEMENT OF TERMS

Insert the address of the property to be let.

The PROPERTY (hereinafter called 'the Property') ______________________________

[1]Delete as applicable. The room must be identified in the Agreement.

The DESIGNATED ROOM[1] ______________________________

The Landlord should give here an address in England or Wales.

The LANDLORD (hereinafter called 'the Landlord') ______________________________

of ______________________________

This is the Landlord's address for service of notices until the Tenant is notified of a different address in England or Wales.

Insert full name(s), and address(es) (if relevant) of every Tenant.

The TENANT (hereinafter called 'the Tenant') ______________________________

of ______________________________

Where the Tenant consists of more than one person, they will all have joint and several liability under this Agreement (this means that they will each be liable for all sums due under this Agreement, not just liable for a proportionate part).

Insert the date the Term begins.

The TERM A periodic tenancy from and including ____________ and continuing month to month until terminated in accordance with this Agreement.

[2] Delete as applicable. NB if rent is paid weekly, a rent book must be provided to the Tenant.

The RENT £__________ per calendar **[month][week]**[2]

by way of standing order into the Landlord's bank, details of which have been provided to the Tenant.[2]

[3] If paid weekly, give the day in the week, e.g. Monday.

The PAYMENT DATE The first payment to be made on the signing of this Agreement. All subsequent payments to be made **[monthly][weekly]**[2] in advance on the **[_________day of the month][______________ of each week]**[2,3].

Information about the tenancy deposit schemes can be obtained from their websites: The Deposit Protection Service at www.depositprotection.com, Tenancy Deposit Solutions Ltd at www.mydeposits.co.uk, and The Dispute Service Ltd at www.thedisputeservice.co.uk. Enter name and telephone number of scheme used. The Deposit must not exceed five weeks' rent.

The DEPOSIT £__________ which will be registered with the following Government authorised tenancy deposit scheme ('the Tenancy Deposit Scheme') in accordance with the Tenancy Deposit Scheme Rules:

____

Tel. ______________________________

Required by paragraph 5 of the Schedule to the Written Statement Regulations 2026, this date should be the same date as the start of the Term

The COMMENCEMENT DATE the tenant is first entitled to take possession of the Property on ___________

Delete this section if there is no Inventory.

The INVENTORY Being the list of the Landlord's possessions at the Property and a schedule of condition of the Property, its fixtures and fittings, which has been signed by the Landlord and the Tenant, a copy of which is annexed hereto.

[4]Delete as applicable, depending on whether whole property or room is being let.

THIS TENANCY AGREEMENT comprises the particulars detailed above and the terms and conditions printed overleaf whereby the **[Property][Designated Room, with a licence, in common with other occupiers of the Property, to make use of such Common Parts as the Landlord may from time to time designate to the Tenant in writing]**[4] is hereby let by the Landlord and taken by the Tenant for the Term at the Rent.

Terms and Conditions

This Agreement is intended to create an Assured Periodic Tenancy as defined in the Housing Act 1988, as amended by the Renters' Rights Act 2025, and the provisions for the recovery of possession by the Landlord in that Act apply accordingly.

[Under this Agreement the Tenant will have an exclusive tenancy of his Designated Room and will have a licence, in common with any other occupier of the Property, to use such Common Parts of the Property as are not exclusively let to other Occupiers and subject to any other restrictions as the Landlord may from time to time notify to the Tenant in writing.][1]

1. The Tenant's obligations:

1.1 To pay the Rent at the times and in the manner aforesaid.

1.2 [To pay all charges in respect of any electric, gas, water, telephonic and televisual services used at or supplied to the Property and Council Tax.] [To make a proportionate contribution to the costs of all charges in respect of any electric, gas, water and telephone or televisual services used at or supplied to the Property and Council Tax.][2]

1.3 To keep the items on the Inventory (if any) and the interior of the Property in a good and clean state and condition and not damage or injure the Property or the items on the Inventory (fair wear and tear excepted).

1.4 To yield up the Property and the items on the Inventory (if any) at the end of the tenancy in the same clean state and condition it/they was/were in at the beginning of the tenancy (but the Tenant will not be responsible for fair wear and tear caused during normal use of the Property and the items on the Inventory).

1.5 Not to make any alteration or addition to the Property and not without the prior written consent of the Landlord (consent not to be withheld unreasonably) do any redecoration or painting of the Property.

1.6 Not do anything on or at the Property which:

1.6.1 may be or become a nuisance or annoyance to any other occupiers of the Property or owners or occupiers of adjoining or nearby premises

1.6.2 is illegal or immoral

1.6.3 may in any way affect the validity of the insurance of the Property and the items listed on the Inventory or cause an increase in the premium payable by the Landlord.

1.6.4 will cause any blockages in the drainage system and in the case of breach of this clause the Tenant to be responsible for the reasonable cost of such repair or other works which will be reasonably required.

1.7 The Tenant may keep a pet at the Property if the Tenant obtains the prior written consent of the Landlord (such consent not to be unreasonably withheld). The Tenant's request for consent under this clause must be made in writing and include a description of the pet or animal.

1.8 Not do or fail to do anything which will lead to the landlord being in breach of any licence granted under Part 2 or Part 3 of the Housing Act 2004.

1.9 To use the Property as a private residence for the Tenant and such other occupiers as the Landlord has expressly permitted only. The Tenant is not to have any other lodgers or long-term guests at the Property without the Landlord's express consent and is not to commit any action that would lead to the Landlord being in breach of any obligation regarding the licensing of the Property as a House of Multiple Occupation pursuant to Part 2 of the Housing Act 2004.

1.10 If the Property is in England, to ensure at all times that all adults residing in the Property have a Right to Rent as set out in Part 3, Immigration Act 2014. The Tenant shall be responsible for carrying out Right to Rent checks with respect to any sub-tenants, lodgers or long-term guests, whether their presence is permitted by the Landlord or not.

1.11 Not to sublet, charge or part with or share possession or occupation of the Property.

1.12 Not to assign the tenancy without the Landlord's consent which will not be unreasonably withheld or delayed. The Landlord may ask the Tenant to enter into a guarantee agreement in respect of any assignee.

1.13 To allow the Landlord or anyone with the Landlord's written permission to enter the [Property][Designated Room][3] at reasonable times of the day to inspect its condition and state of repair, carry out any necessary repairs and gas inspections, show the Property to prospective new tenants, provided the Landlord has given 24 hours prior written notice (except in emergency) [and to further permit the Landlord to freely access the Common Parts of the Property at any time][4].

1.14 To pay the Landlord's reasonable costs reasonably incurred as a result of any breaches by the Tenant of his obligations under this Agreement.

1.15 To pay interest at the rate of 3% above the Bank of England base rate from time to time prevailing on any rent or other money lawfully due from the Tenant which remains unpaid for more that 14 days, interest to be paid from the date the payment fell due until payment.

1.16 To provide the Landlord with a forwarding address when the tenancy comes to an end and to remove all rubbish and all personal items (including the Tenant's own furniture and equipment) from the Property before leaving.

1.17 Not to tamper with any smoke or fire alarm fitted by the Landlord, and to ensure that any batteries in said alarms are replaced as required, and to test said alarms not less than once every calendar month and to promptly report any defect in the alarms to the Landlord.

1.18 To keep any garden tidy and in good condition, carrying out any pruning, lopping, mowing of the lawn, weeding or other such garden maintenance as might be expected of a reasonable tenant.

2. The Landlord's obligations:

2.1 The Landlord agrees that the Tenant may live in the [Property][Designated Room][3] without unreasonable interruption from the Landlord or any person rightfully claiming under or in trust for the Landlord.

2.2 To insure the Property and the items listed on the Inventory and use all reasonable efforts to arrange for any damage caused by an insured risk to be remedied as soon as possible and to provide a copy of the insurance policy to the Tenant if requested.

2.3 To the extent required by section 9A of the Landlord and Tenant Act 1985, the Landlord shall ensure that the Property is fit for human habitation.

2.4 To keep in repair:

2.4.1 the structure and exterior of the Property (including drains, gutters and external pipes)

2.4.2 the installations at the Property for the supply of water, sewage, gas and electricity and for sanitation (including basins, sinks, baths and sanitary conveniences), and

2.4.3 the installations at the Property for space heating and heating water.

2.5 In accordance with regulation 36 of the Gas Safety (Installation and Use) Regulations 1998 (SI 1998/2451), the Landlord shall:

2.5.1 ensure that any relevant gas fitting and any flue that serves a relevant gas fitting is maintained in a safe condition;

2.5.2 ensure that each appliance and flue is checked for safety at the intervals required by the Gas Safety (Installation and Use) Regulations 1998 (SI 1998/2451) by a person approved by the Health and Safety Executive (or an employee of such a person); and

2.5.3 ensure that a record is made of any checks carried out and, subject to exceptions, provide a copy of the record to the Tenant.

2.6 In accordance with regulation 3 of the Electrical Safety Standards in the Private Rented Sector and Social Rented Sector (England) Regulations 2020 (SI 2020/312), the Landlord shall:

[1] Delete paragraph if whole property is being let.

[2] Delete sentence which does not apply.

[3] Delete wording in square brackets that does not apply.

[4] Delete if the Property is being let as a whole.

2.6.1 ensure that the relevant electrical safety standards are met during any period when the Property is occupied under the tenancy;

2.6.3 ensure that relevant electrical installations in the Property are inspected and tested by a qualified person at least every five years or, if required by the most recent report, earlier; and

2.6.4 obtain a report from the person conducting the inspection and test and supply a copy of the report to the Tenant. The report must give the results of the inspection and test and state the date by which the next inspection and test is required.

2.7 But the Landlord will not be required to:

2.7.1 carry out works for which the Tenant is responsible by virtue of his duty to use the Property in a tenant-like manner

2.7.2 reinstate the Property in the case of damage or destruction if the insurers refuse to pay out the insurance money due to anything the Tenant has done or failed to do

2.7.3 rebuild or reinstate the Property in the case of destruction or damage of the Property by a risk not covered by the policy of insurance effected by the Landlord.

2.8 If the Property is a flat or maisonette within a larger building then the Landlord will be under similar obligations for the rest of the building but only in so far as any disrepair will affect the Tenant's enjoyment of the Property and in so far as the Landlord is legally entitled to enter the relevant part of the larger building and carry out the required works or repairs.

2.9 To promptly repair or replace any smoke or fire alarm installed by him at the Property which is reported by the Tenant as being defective.

2.10 If section 190 of the Equality Act 2010 (improvements to let dwelling houses) applies, it has the effect that the Landlord may not unreasonably withhold consent to an application by the Tenant to make an improvement (as defined in section 190(9) of the Equality Act 2010) to the Property where:

(a) a disabled person (as defined in section 6 of the Equality Act 2010) occupies or intends to occupy the premises as their only or main home; and

(b) the improvement is likely to facilitate the disabled person's enjoyment of the premises, having regard to their disability.

The rights and obligations conferred by section 190 of the Equality Act 2010 do not apply in so far as provision of a like nature is made by the tenancy.

3. Ending this Agreement

3.1 If at any time

3.1.1 any part of the Rent is outstanding for 14 days after becoming due (whether formally demanded or not) and/or

3.1.2 there is any breach, non-observance or non-performance by the Tenant of any covenant and/or other term of this Agreement which has been notified in writing to the Tenant and the Tenant has failed within a reasonable period of time to remedy the breach and/or pay reasonable compensation to the Landlord for the breach and/or

3.1.3 any of the grounds contained in the Housing Act 1988 Schedule 2 apply (the Landlord hereby gives the Tenant prior notice of its wish to be able to recover possession on grounds 1B, 2ZA to 2ZD, 4, 5 to 5H, 6A and 18 in Schedule 2 to the Housing Act 1988) and/or

3.1.4 the Tenant is declared bankrupt or enters into an arrangement with some or all of his creditors

the Landlord may recover possession of the Property and this Agreement shall come to an end, subject to the Landlord complying with the proper legal procedure. The Landlord retains all his other rights in respect of the Tenant's obligations under this Agreement. Note that if possession of the Property has not been surrendered and anyone is living at the Property or if the tenancy is an Assured or Assured Periodic Tenancy then the landlord must obtain a court order for possession before re-entering the Property. This clause does not affect the Tenant's rights under the Protection from Eviction Act 1977.

3.2 The Tenant shall give not less than two months' notice in writing to end the Agreement. The notice must expire at the end of a rental period.

3.3 When the tenancy ends, the Tenant shall be entitled to be repaid any part of the Rent that relates to days falling after the end of the tenancy.

4. The Deposit

4.1 The Deposit will be held in a stakeholder capacity in accordance with the Tenancy Deposit Scheme Rules as issued by the relevant Tenancy Deposit Scheme.

4.2 No interest will be payable to the Tenant by the Landlord in respect of the Deposit save as provided by the rules of the relevant Tenancy Deposit Scheme.

4.3 Subject to any relevant provisions of the rules of the relevant Tenancy Deposit Scheme, the Landlord shall be entitled to claim from the Deposit the reasonable cost of any repairs or damage to the Property or its contents caused by the Tenant (including any damage caused by the Tenant's family and visitors) and for any rent in arrears and for any other financial losses suffered or expenditure incurred by the Landlord as a result of the Tenant's breach of these terms and conditions, provided the sum claimed by the Landlord is reasonably incurred and is reasonable in amount. The Landlord is not entitled to claim in respect of any damage to the Property or its contents which is due to 'fair wear and tear' i.e. which is as a result of the Tenant and his family (if any) living in the property and using it in a reasonable and lawful manner.

4.4 As soon as is practicable at the end of the tenancy, the Landlord should inform the Tenant whether any deductions are proposed.

4.5 If there is no dispute, the Deposit will be allocated according to the deductions agreed. If agreement cannot be reached, any of the parties can refer the matter to the relevant Tenancy Deposit Scheme for adjudication.

4.6 If the Tenant comprises more than one individual, each of them agrees with the other(s) that any one of them may consent on behalf of all the others to use alternative dispute resolution through a Tenancy Deposit Scheme to deal with any dispute about the Deposit at the end of the tenancy.

5. Other provisions

5.1 The Landlord hereby notifies the Tenant under Section 48 of the Landlord & Tenant Act 1987 that any notices (including notices in proceedings) should be served upon the Landlord at the address stated with the name of the Landlord overleaf.

5.2 The Landlord shall be entitled to have and retain keys for all the doors to the Property but shall not be entitled to use these to enter the [Property][Designated Room][5] without the consent of the Tenant (save in an emergency) or as otherwise provided in this Agreement.

[5] *Delete wording in square brackets that does not apply.*

5.3 Any notices or other documents (including any court claim forms in legal proceedings) shall be deemed served on the Tenant during the tenancy by either being left at the Property or by being sent to the Tenant at the Property by first-class post. Notices shall be deemed served on the day of hand delivery if before 4 p.m. and otherwise on the next day, or the second working day after posting.

5.4 Any person other than the Tenant who pays all or part of the Rent due under this Agreement to the Landlord shall be deemed to have made such payment as agent for and on behalf of the Tenant which the Landlord shall be entitled to assume without enquiry.

5.5 Any personal items left behind at the end of the tenancy after the Tenant has vacated (which the Tenant has not removed in accordance with clause 1.16 of this Agreement) shall be considered abandoned if they have not been removed within 14 days of written notice to the Tenant from the Landlord or if the Landlord has been unable to trace the Tenant by taking reasonable steps to do so. After this period the Landlord may remove or dispose of the items as he thinks fit. The Tenant shall be liable for the reasonable disposal costs which may be deducted from the proceeds of sale (if any), and the Tenant shall remain liable for any balance. Any net proceeds of sale to be returned to the Tenant at the forwarding address provided to the Landlord.

5.6 In the event of destruction to the Property or of damage to it which shall make the same or a substantial portion of the same uninhabitable, the Tenant shall be relieved from paying the Rent by an amount proportional to the extent to which the Tenant's ability to live in the Property is thereby prevented, save where the destruction or damage has been caused by any act or default by the Tenant or where the Landlord's insurance cover has been adversely affected by any act or omission on the part of the Tenant.

5.7 The Tenant confirms that the Landlord supplied him with a certificate complying with the Energy Performance of Buildings (Certificates and Inspections)(England and Wales) Regulations 2007 prior to the Tenant entering into this Agreement and that the Landlord has supplied him with a certificate complying with the Gas Safety (Installation and Use) Regulations 1998. If the Property is in England the Tenant confirms that the Landlord has supplied him with a copy of the document entitled 'How to Rent: the Checklist for Renting in England'.

5.8 If the Landlord proposes an increase in the Rent, the Landlord must serve a notice in accordance with section 13 of the Housing Act 1988.

5.9 Where the context so admits:

5.9.1 The 'Landlord' includes the persons from time to time entitled to receive the Rent.

5.9.2 The 'Tenant' includes any persons deriving title under the Tenant.

5.9.3 The 'Property' includes any part or parts of the Property and all of the Landlord's fixtures and fittings at or upon the Property.

5.9.4 All references to the singular shall include the plural and vice versa and any obligations or liabilities of more than one person shall be joint and several (this means that they will each be liable for all sums due under this Agreement, not just liable for a proportionate part) and an obligation on the part of a party shall include an obligation not to allow or permit the breach of that obligation.

5.9.5 All references to 'he', 'him' and 'his' shall be taken to include 'she', 'her' and 'hers'.

5.9.6 Any clause requiring the Tenant to do or not do something in relation to the Property should be read as requiring the Tenant to do or not do that same thing in relation to the Designated Room and includes an obligation on the Tenant to use his reasonable endeavours to ensure that no other person does or fails to do that same thing.

5.9.7 The 'Stakeholder' means that the Deposit is held by the Landlord as a neutral party pending the agreement on its payment at the end of the tenancy.

Additional provisions (if any) ____________________

____

____

____

____

____

____

____

____

Signed and executed as a Deed by the following parties:

Landlord

____

____

____

____

Landlord(s)' name(s)

____

____

____

____

Landlord(s)' signature(s)

In the presence of:

Witness signature ____________________

Full name ____________________

Address ____________________

____

Tenant

____

____

____

____

Tenant(s)' name(s)

____

____

____

____

Tenant(s)' signature(s)

Witness signature ____________________

Full name ____________________

Address ____________________

____

LAWPACK®

Lawpack Premium Residential Letting Kit Supplement

Additional content

As well as the downloads listed in the Kit Manual, the Premium Residential Letting Kit provides the following documents to download:

1. **Tenancy Application Form**

   This should be completed and signed by the tenant, giving the landlord the tenant's consent to take up references.

2. **Guarantor Agreement**

   By using this agreement you can get a third-party to guarantee the tenant's obligations, such as paying the rent.

3. **Inventory and Schedule of Condition**

   Records the contents and condition of the property.

Three steps to access you downloads

1 Type the following web address into your internet browser's address bar:

www.lawpack.co.uk

2 Then click on '**Updates & Downloads'**; then from the list: **'Premium Residential Letting Kit P309'**. Insert the following code, then click **'Enter'**:

P3091211929

3 You will now have access to the documents, as well as information on any minor legal changes that affect the Premium Residential Letting Kit.

LAWPACK®

Do-it-yourself Kit

Residential Letting

Guidance Manual

Important facts about this Lawpack Kit

This Lawpack Kit contains the information, instruction and forms necessary to handle your own residential letting agreement. It is not suitable for commercial or agricultural tenancies.

The forms provided with this Lawpack Kit cover the most common letting situations, but we cannot cater for all circumstances. This Manual is intended for people creating either an Assured Periodic Tenancy in England. An occupation contract for Wales is also provided as a download. This Kit is not suitable for letting property located in Scotland or Northern Ireland.

The information contained in this Lawpack Kit has been carefully compiled from professional sources, but its accuracy is not guaranteed, as laws and regulations may change or be subject to differing interpretations.

Neither this nor any other publication can take the place of a solicitor on important legal matters. This Lawpack Kit is sold with the understanding that the publisher, author and retailer are not engaged in rendering legal services. If legal advice or other expert assistance is required, the services of a competent professional should be sought.

As with any legal matter, common sense should determine whether you need the assistance of a solicitor rather than relying solely on the information and forms in this Lawpack Kit.

We strongly urge you to consult a solicitor if:

- substantial amounts of money are involved;
- you do not understand the instructions or are uncertain how to complete and use a form correctly; or
- what you want to do is not precisely covered by the forms provided.

Note: throughout this Lawpack Kit, for 'he', 'his' and 'him' read 'he or she', 'his or her' and 'him or her'.

Contents

How to use this Lawpack Kit

- ✔ This Lawpack Kit can help you achieve an important legal objective conveniently, efficiently and economically. Nevertheless, it is important for you to use this Lawpack Kit properly if you are to avoid later difficulties.
- ✔ **This Lawpack Kit has been updated to be compliant with the Renters' Rights Act 2025** which is now law and will be implemented in stages, with the first parts applying from 1 May 2026. From that date:
  - Fixed-term Assured Shorthold Tenancies will be abolished and replaced with Assured Periodic tenancies.
  - Tenants must be given mandatory information in writing about the tenancy before the tenancy is entered into, usually as part of the tenancy agreement.
  - Rents can only be increased once per year and only after serving a Section 13 notice
  - No further Section 21 notices can be served.
  - For new tenancies, you may not accept rent before signing an Assured Periodic Tenancy and you may not demand more than a month's rent at a time after the agreement is signed.
  - The Government will ban so-called 'rental bidding wars' by requiring adverts list a rental price and banning landlords from accepting or encouraging offers above this listed rent.
  - New rules will be introduced that prevent discrimination against tenants with children or those in receipt of benefits; for access to any legal updates, see foot of page.
- ✔ Read this Manual carefully. It contains the instructions you need to complete the loose-leaf and downloadable documents provided with this Lawpack Kit. If after thorough examination you decide that your requirements are not met by this Lawpack Kit, or you do not feel confident about writing your own documents, consult a solicitor.
- ✔ Shortened URLs (i.e. website addresses) have been used to truncate otherwise lengthy and awkward text; a shortened URL works the same as the original website address.
- ✔ When completing your documents, do not leave any section blank. If any section is inapplicable, - write 'not applicable' or 'none'. This shows you have not overlooked the section.
- ✔ Always use a pen or type on legal documents, never use a pencil. If you cross out or erase anything you have written on your agreement, have the deletions initialled by the landlord and the tenant.
- ✔ The tenancy agreement should be signed by both parties and dated; once completed and signed, you should provide a photocopy of the original agreement for your tenant. Notices and correspondence should likewise be produced in duplicate and copies kept.
- ✔ You will find a helpful glossary of terms at the end of this Manual. Refer to this glossary if you find unfamiliar terms.
- ✔ Always keep legal documents in a safe place and in a location known to your spouse, family, executor or solicitor.

Up-to-date content and downloads can be obtained online as part of our **'Updates and Downloads'** service. Type the following web address into your internet browser's address bar: **www.lawpack.co.uk**. Then click on **'Updates & Downloads'**, then from the list: **'Residential Letting Kit P209'** and use the registration code below.

REGISTRATION CODE: **P2090911728**

Terms and conditions apply. Please check www.lawpack.co.uk/terms.asp for more information.

Introduction

In England, rented accommodation and the rights of tenants are regulated by numerous Acts of Parliament and statutory instruments. The Acts which regulate the creation of tenancies today are the Housing Act 1988, which was amended by the Housing Act 1996 and by the Renters' Rights Act 2025.

Most tenancies will be 'Assured Periodic Tenancies' (APTs). The Renters' Rights Act 2025 abolishes 'no fault' Section 21 notices. Landlords will still be able to end a tenancy when they have a genuine need, but they will rely on the grounds-based Section 8 notice procedure instead. Should you need to apply to the court, you must provide evidence of the grounds you have relied upon. For some grounds, the court must grant possession if the ground is evidenced, but for others, the judge should weigh up whether it is reasonable to grant possession.

It is against the law to evict a residential tenant unless you have a court order. Lawpack publishes an online Eviction eKit that shows you how to legally evict a tenant – see www.lawpack.co.uk for details.

There are other types of tenancy and occupancy rights that exist; for example, where a landlord is resident at the property or an adjacent property, the housing Acts referred to may not apply. Different considerations will also apply to other types of letting, including: low rents; shops; licensed premises; holiday lets; police, military and social housing; sublet or assigned social housing; homeless people; those on probation or release from prison; asylum seekers; displaced people; shared owners; employees; agricultural workers; limited companies; accommodation on boats; and some lettings by charities. None of these is covered by this Lawpack Kit and you should seek specialist legal advice if you are concerned that any of these situations may apply to you.

This Lawpack Kit provides you with documents that enable you to set up and terminate an Assured Periodic Tenancy. It provides the following:

1. An Assured Periodic Tenancy agreement for letting a whole house or flat, or letting individual rooms where tenants in a house or flat will share common parts (such as a kitchen and bathroom).
2. A notice you can use to end the tenancy if your tenant falls into arrears of rent (a notice under section 8 of the Housing Act 1988).
3. This Manual, to help you set up the tenancy and to give you some basic information.

The tenancy agreement will not be suitable if:

- you wish to give a new form of tenancy agreement to an existing tenant who originally went into the property before January 1989; or
- you are or will be resident at the property yourself; this definition includes living in self-contained accommodation in a converted house, but not a purpose-built block;
- there will be an annual rent of more than £100,000; or
- there will be an annual rent of less than £250 (£1,000 in Greater London).

The information and agreement contained in this Lawpack Kit will allow you to grant a simple Assured Periodic Tenancy in England, but this Lawpack Kit does not claim to be comprehensive. Should you require further information on lettings, seek legal advice.

Letting the whole or part of a property

The tenancy agreement forms in this Lawpack Kit can be used in two general circumstances:

1 if you are letting a house or flat as a whole to either one or several tenants; or

2 if you are letting out individual rooms in a shared house or flat, where the tenant has exclusive occupation of part of the property (e.g. his own bedroom) and shares the rest of the property with the other tenants. Normally, this type of agreement will have one tenant only, however couples may sometimes wish to share a room in a shared house.

What are the advantages and disadvantages of each?

Whole house or flat

Advantages

There is only one agreement for the whole property, which reduces paperwork.

If there is more than one tenant, they all have what is called 'joint and several liability' for the whole of the rent. This means that if one of them fails to pay his share, the landlord is entitled to recover this from the other tenants—and will be entitled to get a County Court Judgment against them if they fail to pay.

General administration is simpler and easier from the landlord's point of view.

All bills can be put into the names of the tenants.

Disadvantages

There may be problems if one of the tenants decides to leave before the others. Although the other tenants are liable for the whole of the rent, there may be difficulties in getting them to pay this, even if you get a County Court Judgment (and most landlords would prefer not to go to court or a tribunal). There may also be problems getting a replacement tenant who is acceptable to both you and to the other tenants.

If the tenants are on Housing Benefit they will be entitled to slightly less each, than if the rooms were let on an individual basis.

Individual rooms

Advantages

If one of the tenants leaves, you have more control over his replacement.

If the tenants are claiming Housing Benefit, they will be able to claim more per room than if the property is let as a whole.

Although there may be more paperwork overall, this system will be easier to administer if you have a number of individual tenants who will be moving in and out at different times from each other, as it will not be necessary to ask all the tenants to sign a new joint agreement every time a tenant changes.

Disadvantages

More paperwork and administration for the landlord.

If one tenant leaves, you cannot claim his rent from the other tenants while a replacement tenant is being found.

There may be problems about the use of the common space if tenants are not compatible.

It may be difficult for household bills (such as electricity) to be put in the name of the tenants, which means that you will be liable for them if the tenant does not pay you.

Where there are multiple tenants on separate agreements the landlord will have the overall liability for paying the Council Tax.

The decision on which type of tenancy to create will depend to a large extent on the type of property being let, the type of tenant you are catering for and local conditions generally.

When completing the tenancy agreement:

- if your tenancy is for the whole house or flat, cross out the 'Designated Room' section. Delete relevant text in the clauses in the terms and conditions, as indicated.
- if your tenancy is for a room in a shared house, on the front page you will need to specify which

part of the property is to be occupied exclusively by the tenant (i.e. the Designated Room) and which parts of the property he is going to share with the other tenants. The Designated Room should either be given a name or number (e.g. 'Room 1', or 'The Blue Room'), or its position in the property be specified (e.g. 'The back bedroom on the first floor'). Regarding the 'Common Parts', these will be presumed to be the parts of the Property which you are not letting to other people. You should provide the Tenant with a letter stating which parts of the Property they are permitted to use by description or simply state 'the rest of the property excluding ....' .You should be careful to be precise in these descriptions. You are permitted by the tenancy agreement to vary the Common Parts that the Tenant has the right to use from time to time by sending them a letter but you cannot use a change in the available rooms to put pressure on the Tenant by denying them basic facilities in order to make them pay rent or move out.

Before completing the agreement, you should read the rest of the notes in this Manual.

Houses in multiple occupation ('HMOs')

Whatever type of tenancy you create, if you are letting to three or more unrelated people (i.e. not of the same family) who share living accommodation, then it is likely that the property will be an HMO: a 'house in multiple occupation'. This is as a result of the Housing Act 2004, which changed the previous definition of an HMO.

The significance of letting a property which is an HMO is that, in addition to the normal legal obligations which landlords have to comply with (discussed later in this Manual), there are additional management regulations that apply just to HMOs; for example, contact details for the landlord or his manager must be made available to all occupiers and be displayed in the property. There are also various provisions regarding fire safety, the general safety of occupiers, and the provision of utility services; for instance, you will need to get all electrical installations inspected every five years by a qualified electrician and obtain a certificate to prove this. This, along with the gas safety certificate (see later in this Manual) must be produced for the local authority within seven days of a written request. Other regulations relate to keeping the common parts and the outside of the property in good order and to the disposal of rubbish. Failure to comply with these regulations is a criminal offence, although tenants/occupiers will also be committing a criminal offence if they fail to cooperate with their landlord or obstruct his arrangements for complying with the regulations.

It has been mandatory for large HMOs with three or more storeys and five or more occupants who do not form a single household, to be licensed in England and Wales since 6 April 2006. From 1 October 2018, the Government extended the scope of mandatory HMO licensing in England so that it applies to HMOs with five or more occupiers living in two or more households regardless of the number of storeys. However, local authorities also have the power to widen the remit of licensing to include smaller properties. If you run an HMO, you should contact your local authority to see what the situation is in your area, and whether you will need to be licensed. You should also ask to go on their mailing list so you can be kept informed of future developments.

There are stringent penalties for non-registration of relevant properties and for breaching licensing conditions, which include unlimited fines. Local authority benefit offices and tenants may be able to apply for 'rent repayment orders' to recover up to 12 months' worth of rent or housing benefit where a landlord of a relevant property has breached licensing requirements.

Further information regarding HMO rules and licensing can be obtained from the Ministry of Housing, Communities & Local Government (www.communities.gov.uk). If you are not certain whether the HMO regulations will apply to your property and/or whether your property needs to be licensed, you should speak to your local authority (either the private housing section or the environmental health section) who will advise you.

HMO Planning Consent

Single households of any size fall into the 'C3' planning class. An HMO will fall into the 'C4' planning class, and the change from C3 to C4 use will require planning consent. However, the General Permitted Development Order allows landlords to change their property from a C3 dwelling house to a C4 HMO without applying for planning permission. That general permission takes effect only in areas where the local authority has not removed the permission by making an 'Article 4 Direction'.

Consult your local authority planning department for more information. Failure to obtain planning consent could lead to prosecution.

Landlord registration

There is currently no national landlord registration scheme. However, from late 2026 the Renters' Rights Act will introduce a new Private Rented Sector Database. All landlords of APTs will be legally required to register themselves and their properties on the database and could be subject to penalties if they market or let out a property without registering it and providing the required information.

Individual local authorities are currently entitled to operate landlord licensing schemes under the Housing Act 2004. These work in a similar way to HMO licensing schemes, but they apply to all landlords renting property in a specified area. At the time of writing several areas including Salford, Hastings and various London Boroughs have extensive schemes, but you should check with your local authority to ensure that there is not a scheme which applies to your property.

Tenant referencing

One of the most important things landlords need to do before the start of a tenancy is take up references on candidate tenants. By tenant referencing properly, you should avoid troublesome tenants and prevent the ultimate problem of having to evict them. A Tenancy Application Form is available from Lawpack. It is forbidden to require a tenant to pay for their own references.

If you are still concerned about a tenant's ability to meet his obligations, you might want to consider asking the tenant to provide a guarantor, as discussed below. You should also take up references on a potential guarantor.

Looking after your tenant's data

As a landlord you will be holding and processing personal data relating to your tenants. Although there are exceptions, most landlords ought to be registered with the Information Commissioner's Office (ICO). It is simple and inexpensive to register online https://ico.org.uk/.

You should also provide tenants with a statement about how you use and protect their data. This should say what data you collect and why, what you intend to do with it including whether you will give it to third parties, who exactly you are going to give it to, and when it is going to be deleted. You can find further guidance on the ICO website.

Consents before letting

If you have a mortgage or are going to let a leasehold flat, you need to check to see if you need to obtain permission from your mortgage company and/or your landlord before letting. If consent is not obtained, this could have serious consequences, including the lender or landlord terminating your mortgage or taking possession proceedings against you. Your mortgage company or landlord may impose conditions on any letting, such as the type of tenant you may let to, or the minimum rental amount. Needless to say, you should be careful to comply with these restrictions. Normally, you should include any specific requirements in the tenancy agreement as special clauses. The easiest way of doing this would be to require the tenant to keep to the restrictions imposed by the mortgage company or landlord, and make reference to the letter which informs you of the restrictions. You should then append these letters to the tenancy agreement.

Energy Performance Certificates (EPCs)

Landlords are required to provide prospective tenants with an Energy Performance Certificate (EPC). This must be obtained from an accredited Domestic Energy Assessor (there will be a fee involved). To find an Energy Assessor in your area, you can visit www.gov.uk/get-new-energy-certificate. An EPC provides information on the energy efficiency of the property. You do not have to carry out any improvements to your property as a result of any recommendations made by the Energy Assessor, however your property is likely to be more attractive to tenants if it is energy-efficient.

The EPC must be provided free of charge when property particulars are given to prospective tenants, or when they are first shown round the property. At the very latest, it must be provided before the tenancy agreement is signed. Failure to comply with the regulations may result in a penalty charge notice being served, which currently carries a minimum fine of £500.

Since 1 April 2018, new lettings have been subject to a minimum energy efficiency standard. If the EPC rating is below 'E', the landlord may not let the property without taking certain steps, although often this will be limited to registering an exemption; for details see: https://goo.gl/qGF2Rs.

Tenancy deposit schemes

Most landlords will want to take a damage deposit to have a fund on which to draw at the end of the tenancy, should the property need repair or the contents need repairing or replacing. For tenancies signed on or after 1 June 2019, the maximum tenancy deposit is capped at five weeks' rent if the annual rent is less than £50,000, and six weeks' rent if the annual rent is £50,000 or more.

All landlords who take a damage deposit for an Assured Periodic Tenancy, or who grant a new tenancy to a tenant where a damage deposit was taken before 6 April 2007 must arrange for the deposit to be protected under one of the three government-authorised tenancy deposit schemes. There are two types of scheme:

1. Custodial scheme

This is where the landlord must pass the deposit money over to the scheme administrators, who will hold it during the period of the tenancy. This type of scheme is free of charge (the running costs are paid by the interest earned on the deposit money). Since 1 April 2016, all of the government approved tenancy deposit schemes offer a custodial scheme. The schemes available are:

(i) Deposit Protection Service – www.depositprotection.com; tel 0330 303 0030

(ii) MyDeposits – www.mydeposits.co.uk; tel 0333 321 9401

(iii) Tenancy Deposit Scheme – www.tenancydepositscheme.com; tel 0300 037 1000

2. Insurance-based schemes

This is where the landlord is entitled to hold the deposit money. However, the landlord will have to pay a fee to the scheme administrators and comply strictly with the scheme rules. The scheme administrators have to have insurance cover in place to protect them if the landlord fails to pay over the money, in which case they have to pay the tenant themselves.

All the above three providers offer an insurance-based scheme.

There are three insurance-based schemes. MyDeposits is sponsored by the National Landlords Association and is aimed mainly at landlords; see www.mydeposits.co.uk, tel 0844 980 0290. The scheme run by Tenancy Deposit Scheme is supported by the Association of Residential Lettings Agents, the National Association of Estate Agents and the Royal Institution of Chartered Surveyors. It is aimed mainly at lettings agents; they also offer a scheme in conjunction with the Residential Landlords Association (RLA) called DepositGuard, which operates in the same way as the main Dispute Service scheme and has the same contact details. For further information, contact the scheme administrators direct.

The procedure under the schemes

You should complete the deposit section of the tenancy agreement, to show the amount of the deposit. You are then required under the regulations to provide the tenant with certain prescribed information within 30 days of the deposit having been paid to you. With the MyDeposits scheme you will be sent a form which you must sign and then send on to the tenants. You must also download and supply the MyDeposits leaflet for tenants. This must be done within 30 days of receiving the deposit. If you use the Deposit Protection Service, The Dispute Service, or DepositGuard schemes, you must download and complete the prescribed information form found on their respective websites. You must then sign this form and give it to your tenants.

Failure to register the deposit and supply the correct information to the tenant within 30 days of receipt of the deposit can have severe financial consequences. The forms that you sign have a space for the tenant to sign as well. The tenant does not have to sign the form and it will not be invalid if he declines to do so. It is important that you give the tenant the additional prescribed information, properly completed, from the relevant scheme website – just protecting the deposit is not enough.

You are not required to update the scheme you are using or serve the information again each time you renew the tenancy or when the tenancy continues on a periodic basis as long as:

- The tenant, landlord and premises remain the same; and
- The deposit is held in the same scheme.

At the end of the tenancy you should try to agree with the tenant whether any deductions should be made from the deposit and if so, how much. Most of the deposit protection schemes require you to notify the tenant within ten days of the end of the tenancy if you wish to make deductions from the deposit. Hopefully, the property will have been left in a good condition and you will be able to repay all the deposit to the tenants. If agreement can be reached:

- for deposits protected under the custodial scheme, you will need to inform the scheme administrators and follow the procedure prescribed under their rules;
- for deposits protected under one of the insurance-based schemes, you should pay the money to the tenants and inform the scheme administrators in accordance with the scheme rules that the tenancy has now ended.

If you are unable to reach agreement with the tenant, you should inform the scheme administrators and follow the procedure laid down under their rules. If you are holding the money under one of the insurance-based schemes, you will also have to pay to the scheme administrators the part of the deposit which is in dispute. The other part should be paid to the tenant or kept by you as agreed between you.

The dispute will then be referred to the scheme's adjudicators. You can, if you wish, have the dispute decided by a County court; however, this is not advisable as it will take far longer to resolve and will involve court fees. The adjudication service provided under the deposit protection schemes is free of charge.

You will need to provide full details of your claim under the damage deposit to the adjudicator together with a copy of the tenancy agreement, a copy of the inventory and any other evidence of the condition of the property, such as photographs. Note that although an inventory is not mandatory under the deposit protection schemes, your chances of success in an adjudication will be very slight if you do not have one. You can purchase a Property Inventory at www.lawpack.co.uk. You will also be expected to provide invoices for all repair and other work done, and receipts for replacement items purchased, and any other expenses you may have incurred which you are claiming from the tenant. The adjudicator will not seek further evidence from you if you do not provide these initially. Therefore, you must ensure that you provide full evidence, including receipts, quotes and estimates, for all amounts you are claiming.

The adjudicator will then normally decide the case based on the paperwork. The deposit money will be paid by the scheme administrators in accordance with the adjudicator's decision within 10 days of being informed of it. The possibility of appeal from the adjudicator's decision is very limited. You may complain to the scheme if you believe that the adjudicator has not followed the procedure properly; if this is unsatisfactory, you may be able to seek judicial review of the decision in the High Court. However, this will only be possible in the most extreme cases.

If the tenant disappears at the end of the tenancy leaving no forwarding address, you should contact the scheme administrators and follow the rules for the particular scheme you are using. However, if the tenant left leaving damage and/or rent arrears, you will be able to claim these from the damage deposit, although the case may have to be referred to an adjudicator first.

Non-compliance

- All deposits should be protected in a deposit scheme. No penalty claim can be made in relation to a deposit taken before 6 April 2007 unless a new tenancy agreement (or renewal document) is given to the tenant after 6 April 2007. However, no Section 8 notice can be served by a landlord who has not protected a deposit, whenever taken.
- If you take a deposit for an Assured Periodic Tenancy that is not protected under one of the schemes or where the deposit is protected but the prescribed information has not been served, your tenants can go to court asking for:
  (a) the deposit to be returned to them; or
  (b) the deposit to be protected under the custodial scheme; and
  (c) an order that you pay them a sum up to three times the amount of the deposit money, within 14 days.
- Note also that you will not be entitled to gain possession of the property while the deposit is not protected under one of the statutory schemes.

Avoiding tenancy deposit protection

Some landlords are unhappy about using the tenancy deposit protection scheme and seek alternatives to taking a deposit which will be subject to it. Generally, these alternatives are unsatisfactory. Below are some of the ways that landlords have tried to avoid the tenancy deposit scheme:

- Taking a deposit which is not money. This is specifically prohibited under the Housing Act 2004.
- Taking a guarantee. As no money changes hands, guarantees are not subject to the tenancy deposit protection scheme rules. If the guarantee is from a local authority under one of their bond schemes, this is an excellent alternative. However, a guarantee taken from a friend or relative of the tenant may be less satisfactory. The guarantor may prove difficult to find when the money is needed, or may refuse to pay, making time-consuming County court proceedings necessary. If it turns out that the guarantor has no assets, it may be difficult to enforce this.
- Taking two months' rent in advance instead of a month's rent and a deposit. This seems superficially satisfactory, as the tenant will normally pay the same amount of money at the start. However, as the money is for rent rather than damage, it cannot be used for anything other than rent, and the landlord will be left without a fund for damages at the end of the tenancy. Be warned also that in each case the Court will consider the situation and may well consider rent paid in advance to be a deposit, which requires protection.

- Insurance-based alternatives. These have been developed by some insurance companies. Generally, they will only be available where tenants have passed the insurance companies' referencing procedure, so cannot normally be used for the tenants most likely to cause problems.
- Putting up the rent instead of taking a deposit. This is a valid option, however it may make the property less attractive to tenants.
- Finally, you may decide not to take any deposit at all.

Note that the alternatives discussed above do not give the tenant the incentive to look after the property that the prospect of losing their deposit will provide. In practice, most of the methods of avoiding the system are probably more trouble than simply registering the deposit as required.

Inventory and schedule of condition

As mentioned above, having a proper detailed inventory of the property's condition and contents is important – landlords will find it difficult to make any recovery from the damage deposit if one is not done.

You can purchase a Property Inventory from Lawpack Publishing at www.lawpack.co.uk. You should go through the house room by room, noting on the inventory all the items in each room. Even if you are letting a property unfurnished, it is a good idea to have an inventory to record the condition of the walls and carpets, etc., in case of future dispute. You should also make a note of the condition of the items on the inventory (e.g. a stain on a carpet or rug), so that the tenant cannot assert that the damage they have caused existed at the start of the tenancy.

The inventory should be checked with the tenant before he moves into the property – the 'check-in'. You then retain the signed copy of the inventory which you should copy for your tenants to assist them at the end of the tenancy. One copy per property is sufficient.

When the tenant is about to leave, the landlord (or his agent) should meet him at the property and go through the inventory with him again (the 'check-out'), room by room. If there are any missing or damaged items, it is often possible to sort out how much should be deducted from the damage deposit there and then.

If you do not want to prepare an inventory, you can delete the inventory section on the first page of the tenancy agreement. However, we strongly recommend that an inventory be prepared for all agreements. Even if the property is let unfurnished, an Inventory can contain useful information about the condition of doors and windows, the paintwork, light fittings and carpets.

Whether or not you are preparing an inventory, it is a good idea to take photos of all areas of the property, ensuring that photographs are dated. With a digital camera this is particularly easy and it is simple to place all the photographs on a CD and to give it to the tenant at the start of the tenancy. Carrying out a similar process at the end will help supplement the tenancy with strong visual evidence of the condition of the property. This process works especially well for gardens which are particularly hard to describe effectively in an inventory.

If you do not have time to prepare an inventory yourself, there are many professional inventory clerks who can do this for you, for a fee. You can locate some from The Association of Independent Inventory Clerks (AIIC) who have a website at www.theaiic.co.uk.

According to the Tenant Deposit Scheme (TDS) the most common cause of deposit dispute between landlords and tenants is property cleanliness at check-out stage. The other main areas of dispute are property damage, redecoration, rent arrears and garden maintenance. The AIIC considers the most common cleaning problems at check-out to be: dirty ovens, stained and marked carpets, limescale on kitchen and bathroom fittings, kitchen surface grease marks, and thick dust and cobwebs. It is worth highlighting these points to your tenant a week or two before the end of the tenancy, to encourage them to make sure the property is clean and avoid the resulting disputes.

Guarantor

If you are worried about a prospective tenant's ability to pay the rent, it might be wise to take a guarantee from a third party guarantor; for example, guarantees are often taken from the parents of students when they sign tenancy agreements. However, you should take up references and do credit checks on guarantors, as you would on a tenant; it is no good having a guarantor who is as impecunious as a tenant. A rent guarantee agreement is available at www.lawpack.co.uk.

Terms in the tenancy agreement

One of the main reasons for having a form of tenancy agreement is to set out the landlord's and tenant's obligations to each other, known by lawyers as 'covenants'. Having a clear and comprehensive tenancy agreement can help prevent future disputes.

In this Lawpack Kit there is an Assured Periodic Tenancy agreement; the main terms are on the front page and standard terms in the middle two pages. You should read these carefully. Once completed and signed, you should provide a photocopy of the original agreement for your tenant.

Date of agreement: The agreement should be dated on the date that everyone signs it (or if signing on different dates, the date of the last signatory). If the agreement is signed and dated before the date on which the tenancy is to start, it is important that the signatures are properly witnessed.

The property address: It is also useful to add here details of any garages or additional parking.

The designated room: Applies only if your tenancy is for individual rooms. Delete if not applicable.

The landlord's address: It is important that the agreement gives an address for the landlord in England or Wales. This is because section 48 of the Landlord and Tenant Act 1987 provides that the rent does not have to be paid until an address in England or Wales for the service of notices and documents has been provided to the tenant. If the landlord is resident abroad or living in Scotland, there should always be a contact address given in England or Wales. If this is not possible, the landlord should consider using a letting agency.

The tenant: Make sure that all the tenants are listed on the agreement and that they all sign the agreement.

The commencement date: This is the date on which the tenancy begins..

The tenancy can start on the same date or after the date on which it is signed and dated, in which case it is important that the signatures are properly witnessed.

The rent: If the rent is too high, it may be subject to challenge.

Lawpack's Rent Book is available from stationers or www.lawpack.co.uk.

Banned fees

You must avoid charging any banned fees.

Landlords may not charge the tenant any fee or charge other than: the rent; a holding deposit (up to one week's rent and repayable to the tenant in most circumstances); a tenancy deposit (capped at five weeks' rent if the annual rent is less than £50,000, and six weeks' rent if the annual rent is £50,000 or more) or one of a handful of other permitted payments. You may require the tenant to pay for the utilities (including telephone and internet). If the tenant breaches the agreement you may demand compensation from them, but 'penalty charges' are prohibited and will not be enforceable. You may impose reasonable charges if the tenant wishes to end the tenancy early, or for dealing with a variation of the tenancy agreement, an assignment, or a 'change of sharer' (swapping one of the joint tenants).

Under the Renters' Rights Act 2025, rent in advance is restricted in several ways. Landlords may not demand, encourage, or accept rent payments in advance before agreeing to enter into an Assured Periodic Tenancy. After the Assured Periodic Tenancy is agreed upon but before the tenant moves in, the landlord/agent may demand up to a month's rent or up to 28 days if the rental period is less than a month (the initial payment of rent).

Landlords are only permitted to increase rents once per year to the market rate – the price that would be achieved if the property was newly advertised to let. To do this, they will need to serve a 'Section 13' notice, setting out the new rent and giving at least 2 months' notice of it taking effect.

Your own terms and conditions

The Lawpack agreements provide a space on the final page for you to put any additional terms and conditions that you would like to have included; for example, you may use it to disallow smoking and the use of e-cigarettes. If the property is for a room in a shared house, you could insert some 'house rules'. It is important that you are as precise as is reasonably possible when writing additional clauses. Try to avoid long words and slang terms and if there is any doubt, repeat the clause in a different way.

In the Assured Periodic Tenancy, terms and conditions in the agreements that are inappropriate can be deleted; all deletions should be initialled by both landlord and tenant(s). You should note, however, that some things are laid down in the housing legislation and cannot be altered. Many other parts of the agreement are there for your protection. You should therefore exercise caution when making deletions; for example, you cannot contract out of your responsibility to keep the structure and exterior of the property and the installations for essential services in proper repair (as set out in clause 2.4 of the Assured Periodic Tenancy agreement). Any clause making the tenant responsible for these things will be void.

Bear in mind that the tenancy agreements are designed to cover most situations. Note also that there are regulations in force (the Consumer Rights Act 2015) which provide that if a term is 'unfair' (e.g. if it seeks to take away the tenant's legal rights or imposes onerous obligations on the tenant during the tenancy, such as excessive cleaning requirements), that term will be void and unenforceable. If you do not know what you are doing when altering tenancy agreement terms, it is easy to invalidate them, particularly if you are making them less favourable to the tenant. Lawpack agreements have been designed to comply with these regulations. If you want to make substantial alterations, you should seek legal advice before doing so.

Witnesses

If the agreement is being signed in advance of the tenancy start date, it is advisable but not essential to have the signatures witnessed. Otherwise, if the tenancy starts immediately and has a market rent, strictly speaking there is no need to have the signatures witnessed, although it is advisable to do so. The witness can be the same person for all of the signatures on the agreement. The witness should be someone independent.

Tenant's obligations

Repairing obligations

Although many repairing obligations are by law down to the landlord, the tenant also has a duty to use the property in a 'tenant-like manner'. This means that he will be responsible for any repairs that are due to his own negligence, even if they would otherwise fall to be paid for by the landlord.

Generally, the tenant is responsible for the condition of the interior of the property. However, you will probably not want, for example, your tenant to paint all the walls black, so clause 1.5 in Lawpack's Assured Periodic Tenancy provides for the landlord's consent to be obtained before any redecoration is done. Note that the clause also provides for the consent 'not to be withheld unreasonably'. This wording is essential to enable the clause to comply with the Consumer Rights Act 2015 and it may become invalid if the wording is deleted. This also applies to any other clauses that contain this wording.

Outgoings

The landlord will not normally want to be stuck paying the tenant's bills, so the agreements provide for the tenant to pay them. This is easier where a property is let as a whole, where you can insist that the tenant registers with the utilities. A template form of letter to service/utility providers regarding the tenant's responsibility for the payment of bills is provided as a download. However, where there is a number of different tenants coming and going on individual tenancy agreements, the utility accounts may have to be in the landlord's name. If there are any accounts that the landlord will pay, for example some landlords pay the water rates, then the tenancy agreement should be altered to show this.

If the property is let on a number of individual agreements, the landlord will be primarily responsible for paying the Council Tax. Check the amount with your local authority, to allow you to take this into account when setting your rent.

Use of the property

It is important that a tenant uses the property solely for residential purposes, as otherwise this may put the landlord in breach of planning regulations and the lease will be of a totally different type. A clause is therefore included regarding this. The landlord will also want to prevent the tenant from letting anyone else live at the property, as he will only want tenants whom he has checked and approved.

Access for the landlord

This is important, as the landlord will need to visit and inspect the property from time to time, to ensure that the property is in good condition, and to do any repairs and gas safety checks. The agreements provide for the landlord to retain keys to the property; however, he should never use these without the tenant's consent, except in an emergency. Accessing the property without the tenant's consent, or in direct contravention of it is a criminal offence and you could go to prison if you do so.

Landlord's obligations

There is a number of obligations that are imposed on a landlord by law and which the landlord cannot avoid. These are summarised below:

England only – 'Right to rent' checks

For all tenancies in England which began on or after 1 February 2016, landlords must check the immigration status of tenants to ensure they have a right to reside in the UK, also known as the 'right to rent'. All landlords will need to check that a prospective tenant has:

- a permanent right to rent, because he is a UK or Ireland national, or he has a permanent right to reside; or
- a time-limited right to rent, because he holds a time limited visa conferring a right to reside in the UK for a period.

Checks only need to be carried out on adults, but all adult occupiers need to be checked. The landlord must:

- conduct initial right to rent checks before signing the tenancy agreement;
- conduct follow-up checks at the appropriate date, if initial checks indicate that an occupier has a time-limited right to rent;
- make a report to the Home Office if follow-up checks indicate that an occupier no longer has the right to rent.

You should obtain original versions of one or more of the acceptable documents for each adult occupier, check the documents in the presence of the holder of the documents, and make copies of the documents and retain them with a record of the date on which the check was made. In simple cases, this will mean seeing the prospective tenant's British or EEA passport in their presence, taking a copy of the passport, and recording when this check was carried out. It is also possible to conduct a right to rent check online if the tenant has certain types of immigration status and provides the landlord with a 'share code'. It is important that you do not carry out checks in a discriminatory way.

A list of the acceptable documents and further guidance about how to carry out checks is at https://goo.gl/FLEV54. If you do not carry out the checks and one of the occupiers does not have the right to rent, you may be liable for fine of up to £20,000 per occupier, or criminal prosecution.

Repairing covenants

Under the Landlord and Tenant Act 1985 the landlord must keep in repair the structure and exterior of the property, and the installations for the supply of services (gas, electricity, water, sanitation, space and water heating). This is set out in clause 2.4 of the Assured Periodic Tenancy agreement. The landlord's obligations extend to the roof of the property, drains and gutters. The property also has to be wind- and watertight and 'fit for human habitation' at the start of and throughout the tenancy.

The Homes (Fitness for Human Habitation) Act 2018 allows tenants to take legal action against their landlord if the property is not fit for human habitation. This adds to the existing right for tenants to force landlords to fix 'disrepair'; a property might be unfit for human habitation because of hazards at the property, even without there being any disrepair.

Landlords must provide their tenants with a copy of the government leaflet *How to rent: the checklist for renting in England* which is available online at https://goo.gl/DPtjZq.

Fire safety, smoke and carbon monoxide alarms

In newer properties, fire detection systems are required to be fitted under the Building Regulations and if these have been fitted, they must be working at the start of the tenancy and kept in repair by the landlord.

The Smoke and Carbon Monoxide Alarm (Amendment) Regulations 2022 came into force on 1 October 2022. From that date, all relevant landlords must:

- ensure at least one smoke alarm is equipped on each storey of their properties where there is a room used as living accommodation. This has been a legal requirement in the private rented sector since 2015.
- ensure a carbon monoxide alarm is equipped in any room used as living accommodation which contains a fixed combustion appliance (excluding gas cookers).
- ensure smoke alarms and carbon monoxide alarms are repaired or replaced once informed and found that they are faulty.

The requirements are enforced by local authorities who can impose a fine of up to £5,000 where a landlord fails to comply with a remedial notice.

Gas safety

Under the Gas Safety Regulations a landlord must have the gas installations at a property inspected annually by an installer registered with the Gas Safe Register, and provide a certificate to this effect to the tenant. You must also provide a copy of the up-to-date certificate before tenants move in, and you should keep evidence to prove that you did. Landlords should check the current regulations with their local health and safety executive, who enforce them. It is a criminal offence not to comply with these regulations. Faulty gas appliances can be lethal and tenants have died as a result of them (and their landlords convicted and imprisoned).

Gas Safety certificates must be renewed annually and landlords usually leave getting a new one as late as possible because the earlier they renew, the earlier the next one will be due. A recent change in the law allows annual checks to be carried out any time between 10 and 12 months after the previous check, without changing the annual renewal date.

Furniture, electrical equipment and general product regulations

These various regulations require furniture to be fire-safety compliant, and all electrical equipment and other items in the property to be safe. Further information about this can be obtained from your local trading standards office, which enforces the regulations. Again, it is a criminal offence not to comply with these regulations.

There is a now a requirement for landlords to obtain an Electrical Installations Condition Report (EICR) at least every five years and to provide a copy to the tenant both when they move into the property and when any new check is done. Except where required by a property licence condition, there is no obligation to perform a portable appliance test, but you may wish to do this anyway.

Covenant of 'quiet enjoyment' and the Protection from Eviction Act

This is a general covenant that is implied in all tenancies, which provides for the tenant to occupy the property without interference ('quiet enjoyment'). It means that the landlord should not enter the property without the tenant's consent (except in an emergency), should keep the property in a proper condition, and should not do anything or allow anyone else to do anything which would affect the tenant's rights under the tenancy agreement or the general law; for example, stopping services to 'persuade' the tenant to leave.

A landlord who lets a number of separate units in a property should note that he also has a duty to his other tenants under the covenant of quiet enjoyment; for example, if one tenant is disruptive, the other tenants will look to the landlord to remedy the situation and if necessary evict the disruptive tenant.

Further obligations are imposed on the landlord under the Protection from Eviction Act 1977 (PEA). It requires that the landlord not harass the tenant or encourage anyone else to do so on their behalf and not enter onto the property without the tenant's consent or a Court order. Breach of the PEA can lead to prosecution. The tenant is also able to take civil proceedings to seek damages from the landlord for their actions. A single action can amount to harassment under the PEA. It is no defence that the tenant is in breach of contract (e.g. by being in arrears of rent). Landlords should note that associated acts such as turning off utilities or blocking access to the property are also deemed harassment under the PEA.

Insurance

A landlord has no obligation to insure the property and its contents but it is something that any responsible landlord would probably wish to do anyway, in order to protect his investment.

A landlord should ensure that the insurance policy he has is suitable for rented property – his normal household insurance generally will not be. Check the terms of the policy carefully, as some policies exclude cover for lettings to some types of tenant. The agreements included in this Lawpack

Kit provide for the landlord to give the tenant a copy of the insurance policy. This is so the landlord can hold the tenant responsible if he does anything that voids the insurance or causes the landlord's premiums to increase.

Tenants are responsible for insuring their own property and this should be made clear to them. However, landlords cannot insist that they do this. It is up to the tenant whether he insures his own property or not.

Rent control

If they feel that the rent of a property is too high, assured periodic tenants have the right to refer the matter to the First-tier Tribunal (Property Chamber); any referral must be made within the first six months of the tenancy.

It is no longer possible to rely on a rent increase clause in a tenancy agreement. Rent can only be increased by the landlord serving a section 13 notice proposing the new rent or a First-tier Tribunal determination of open market rent. Lawpack provides a Rent Increase eForm to assist with this process, which is available from www.lawpack.co.uk.

Landlord's notice to end tenancy

Provided as a downloads with this Lawpack Kit is a Section 8 Notice Seeking Possession under the Housing Act 1988.

It is very important that a landlord's notice is in the correct form, as otherwise the landlord will not be able to use it in court/tribunal proceedings for possession. A letter asking the tenant to leave by a certain date will not be sufficient.

For all notices, the names of the parties and the address should match those in the tenancy agreement (even if some tenants have moved out, they should still be named on the notice if they were named on the most recent tenancy agreement). If the tenant is renting a room in a shared house, you need to specify the room (e.g. 'Room 1') rented by the tenant, as well as the property address. The notices should be completed as follows:

Section 8 Notice based on rent arrears

This notice can be used if the tenant falls into arrears of rent. Under the Housing Act, as amended by the Renters' Rights Act 2025, if the tenant is in arrears of rent of at least three months or more (or 13 weeks for a weekly tenancy) at the date of the service of this notice, and at the date of any court hearing, the landlord is entitled to an order for possession as of right. The notice should not therefore be used until the arrears have reached three months. For example, if the monthly rent is £500 then the rent arrears must be at least £1,500.

This notice must give the tenant a notice period of at least four weeks to sort things out and repay the arrears. When you are calculating the expiry of the notice period you will need to account for at least two working days for service by post.

Service of the notice

It is recommended that whenever possible, these notices are served either by handing them to the tenant personally, or by leaving them at the property, normally by insertion through the letter-box of the property in an envelope addressed to the tenant(s). If you are leaving it for the tenant at the property, it must not be left in a communal post box or table but must be placed in a private box or under the door of the property. If in doubt, it should be taped to the door covering the keyhole and a photograph taken of it.

If you are unable to do this, the tenancy agreement form provides for you to send it by post. Where you are using the post to serve the notice then you should get some evidence of the service by getting a proof of posting which is freely available from the post office. However, unless you trust the tenant to sign and return the copy notice to you to prove it, service by post is not recommended. The reason being that there is no way you can prove (e.g. if you are challenged by a tenant at court saying that he has never received the notice) that it was ever delivered. You can send the notice by recorded delivery, but note that tenants often refuse to accept and sign for recorded delivery items. With a difficult tenant, notices should only ever be served by hand. It you cannot do this yourself, arrange for someone else to serve it for you or arrange for this to be done by a professional process server. If you think the tenant may lie and deny having received the notice, even where it was delivered by hand, use a process server or arrange to have an independent witness present.

Tenants' notice to quit

A tenant will need to give at least two months' notice in writing (which will need to align with the end of a rent period), subject to any shorter period the parties might have agreed (whether in the tenancy agreement or in a separate document).

Landlords are not permitted to specify a particular form of written communication a notice to quit must take.

A tenant's notice to quit premises let under an Assured Periodic Tenancy can be withdrawn before the proposed termination date, if the landlord and tenant agree in writing. This provision enables the parties to agree that the original Assured Periodic Tenancy should simply continue; for example, where the tenant decides that he or she wants to stay at the property after all and the landlord is happy to agree to this.

Eviction

It is important to understand that it is against the law to evict a tenant of residential property by force, or to harass a tenant to make him leave by, for example, cutting off the gas or water supply. If you take steps to evict an occupier without a court order, you could be liable to criminal prosecution (and immediate imprisonment for three months) and/or a claim for damages by the tenant.

A landlord only has a right to evict where the agreement with the tenant contains such a right, and where the landlord is able to rely on one of the 'statutory grounds for possession'. The most important of the statutory grounds is:

- where the tenant is in arrears of rent of more than three months; here also, provided the proper form of notice (the Section 8 Notice) has been served, you are entitled to a possession order as of right (assuming you can establish and prove the grounds for possession).

You can also evict a tenant for other breaches of his tenancy agreement (e.g. antisocial behaviour or damaging the property), although these proceedings will normally be more complex and expensive. However, a landlord should try to deal with any breach of the tenancy agreement without delay.

It is essential that you keep copies of the completed tenancy agreement, any notices served on the tenant (with a record of the date and method of service, the name of the person who served it and any witnesses), and up-to-date records of all correspondence and communications with the tenant. These may later be required as evidence in court/First-tier Tribunal, should you need to apply for a court order for possession.

The law relating to the eviction of tenants through the courts is complex, and it is beyond the scope of this Lawpack Kit to offer more than general guidance. You should consult a solicitor before taking any action. Even if you are relying on one of the grounds for possession that entitle you to a possession order as of right, the court will expect you to follow the correct procedure. Judges consider eviction to be a last resort and will not do so if the landlord has not got his paperwork in order. It is very easy for someone who is unfamiliar with the process to misunderstand the rules and get things wrong.

Checklist

You should now be in a position to decide on the type of tenancy that is most suitable to your circumstances and by referring to the Notes for Guidance on the Lawpack agreement and this Manual, fill the forms in correctly. Use the following checklist to ensure there is nothing that you have forgotten.

1. Check if you require the consent of any third party for the creation of the tenancy. For example, the bank or building society to whom the property is mortgaged, and/or your landlord, if the property is leasehold. If the property is leasehold, you should provide a copy of your lease to the tenant and add the following words in the space for additional terms and conditions on the final page of the agreement:

   'To observe and perform all the terms and conditions contained in any superior lease to which the property is subject, a copy of the lease having been provided to the tenant'.

   If the property is mortgaged, the building society may require the tenant to serve further notices prescribed by it acknowledging the landlord's right to terminate the tenancy agreement and regain possession under Ground 2 of Schedule 2 and Section 7(6) of the 1988 Act. You should check the mortgage lender's requirements. If your lender wants this notice served, it should provide you with a copy of the relevant form.
2. Obtain an Energy Performance Certificate for the property (and if the rating is 'F' or 'G' check whether the minimum energy efficiency standard rules apply). A copy of this must be provided to all tenants when the property particulars are given to them or when they view the property.
3. Check the immigration status of tenants and take up references on behalf of all the tenants who are to be parties to the tenancy agreement, as well as any guarantors. Bank and employer's references are essential. Credit reference agencies can run credit checks against tenants for a small fee. Register with the Information Commissioner's Office and provide tenants with a statement about how you use and protect their data.
4. If there are full-time occupiers of the property aged over 18 years (other than the tenant), for example adult children of the tenant, then ensure that these occupiers are also named as tenants and that they sign the agreement.
5. Many tenants are entitled to receive Housing Benefit from their local authority to assist with their rent. This is a means-tested benefit. For all applications after 8 April 2008, including where there is a break in the claim or the address is changed, this will be provided in the form of a Local Housing Allowance (LEA) paid direct to the tenant. Unlike the old Housing Benefit system (which will still applies to some older tenancies) this cannot normally be paid direct to the landlord. It should only be paid to the landlord directly where the tenant is vulnerable or in rent arrears. The LEA is set by the Rent Officer for the local area, and this will be the sum paid to the tenant, regardless of the rent actually charged by the landlord for the property. Housing Benefit is being gradually replaced by Universal Credit. For more information about the Housing Benefit system and how it works, you should contact your local authority.

   The Renters' Rights Act 2025 prohibits a prospective landlord (or someone acting on their behalf) from discriminating against prospective tenants who would have a child living with them or visiting them.

   The 2025 Act also prohibits a prospective landlord (or someone acting on their behalf) from discriminating against prospective tenants who claim benefits. A prospective landlord must not prevent someone from enquiring about the property, accessing information about the property, viewing the property or taking a tenancy of the dwelling on the basis that the prospective tenant claims benefits. Blanket policies or practices that would have the effect of deterring a tenant who claims benefits are also prohibited.
6. Notify your insurer of the letting.
7. If the property has any gas appliances, arrange for these to be checked by an installer registered

with the Gas Safe Register, and obtain the necessary certificate to give to the tenants. Also ensure that you have the appropriate fire and carbon monoxide detection devices in your property.

10. You are obliged to consider undertaking a legionella risk assessment for the property, although in most cases, a full assessment will not be necessary. See the Health and Safety Executive website for details, at https://goo.gl/lCfgsI.
11. Carefully prepare, check and sign the inventory with the tenant before the tenancy is entered into. It is best to walk through the property with the tenant when doing this.
12. Arrange for the damage deposit (if you take one) to be protected under one of the government authorised tenancy deposit schemes, notify the tenant (using the form provided by your scheme administrators, if any) of the scheme used and prescribed information within 30 days of the deposit being paid to you, and ensure that you comply with the rules of the scheme used by you at all times.
13. Ensure deposit money is collected and has cleared through your bank account before you release the keys to the tenant. Consider setting up a bank standing order with the tenant for the collection of rent payments (the Lawpack tenancy agreement provides for this and a template form of mandate is provided to download).
14. Arrange for the tenancy agreement to be signed and ensure that the signatures are properly witnessed, unless the tenancy is to start immediately. Hand over the gas certificate and any other relevant paperwork such as the Ministry of Housing, Communities and Local Government publication *How to Rent: the checklist for renting in England.*
15. Once completed and signed, you should provide a photocopy of the original tenancy agreement for your tenant.

Glossary

assured tenancy – a tenancy of a dwelling-house granted to an individual as his principal or only home on or after the commencement date of the Housing Act 1988, and being a tenancy to which the Housing Acts 1988 and 1996 apply, whereby the landlord may only regain possession of the property subject to the assured tenancy upon establishing one of the grounds for possession contained in the 1988 Housing Act (as amended) and the tenant therefore has the benefit of full security of tenure protection.

dwelling-house – a home. It can include such units as flats and bedsits. The unit of property that can become the subject of security of tenure under the Housing Act 1988.

determine – a legal term meaning to end.

eviction – the recovery of property from the person in occupation of it.

excluded tenancy or licence – a tenancy or licence where the tenant or licensee has the use of any accommodation in common with the owner or a member of the owner's family, and who occupied the property as his only or principal home both at the beginning and end of the tenancy or licence. Such tenancies and licences are excluded from a number of the provisions preventing possession being recovered without due process of law.

forfeiture – a landlord's common law right to re-enter the property if the tenant is in breach of a covenant in a tenancy agreement. A right to forfeiture can only arise if expressly provided for in the tenancy agreement. There are substantial statutory restraints on the landlord's power to exercise his/her right to forfeiture, including the need to serve certain notices and obtain a court order. Note that possession proceedings based on forfeiture can no longer be used for assured and Assured Periodic Tenancies.

guarantor – a person who promises the performance of contractual obligations by one party to the other in a contracted agreement.

inventory – a detailed list of items, for example, furniture and personal goods.

landlord – the legal owner of a property on which a tenancy has been created.

licence – a personal permission to occupy land whether in exchange for payment or not. This does not give the licensee the rights of a tenant. Note however that you cannot prevent someone (e.g. someone living in a property at a rent) from being a tenant just by calling their occupation a licence, for example by getting them to sign a document headed 'Licence Agreement'.

licensee – a person occupying property with the consent of the owner but without enjoying a legal interest in the property occupied.

licensor – a person who consents to another person occupying his property without giving that person a legal interest in the property.

mortgage – the charging of property by a borrower to a lender as security for debt.

mortgagor – the person charging the property, or borrower.

mortgagee – the person in favour of whom the property is mortgaged, or lender.

notice – a formal and (usually) written warning of an event that is to happen that is delivered in advance of the event by one contracting party to the other contracting party. Many notices have to be in a special form prescribed by statute.

possession – actual and physical control or occupation of property.

security of tenure – the right of a tenant to remain in occupation of property that he does not own, but which he has been granted or has acquired a legal right to occupy. This can sometimes be against the wishes of the legal owner.

tenant – a person who occupies property let by a landlord and has the benefit of a legal interest in the property.

tenancy – the arrangement or agreement under which the tenant occupies the property. A tenancy does not have to be in writing, but oral tenancies have many disadvantages, particularly for the landlord, and should be avoided.

without prejudice – a much-used legal phrase that means 'without affecting any existing rights or remedies'.